# Especially for Husbands

### when was the last time...

**This Book Is a Gift for**

_____

**From**

_____

# Especially for Husbands

### when was the last time...

**MICHAEL A. CAMPION, PH.D.**
**with photographs by Wilmer Zehr**

Bethany Fellowship INC.
MINNEAPOLIS, MINNESOTA 55438

Published by Bethany Fellowship, Inc.
6820 Auto Club Road,
Minneapolis, Minnesota 55438

Printed in the United States of America

ISBN 0-87123-136-0

When it comes to their husbands,
Most women accept the following guideline:

## *Blessed are those who expect nothing for they shall never be disappointed.*

Let's be *real men* and take loving, positive authority over our families. This book was written in an effort to help men by suggesting some positive things they can do to become involved in their homes. Marriage is like a garden in that if you let it run its course, you get weeds (problems). It takes active involvement and planning by the husband to develop a warm, a loving family. This book is not a send-off for a guilt trip but a challenge to action...

# When Was the Last Time...

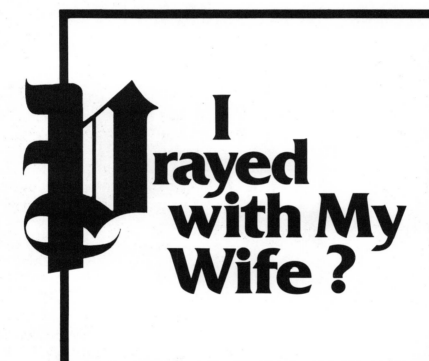

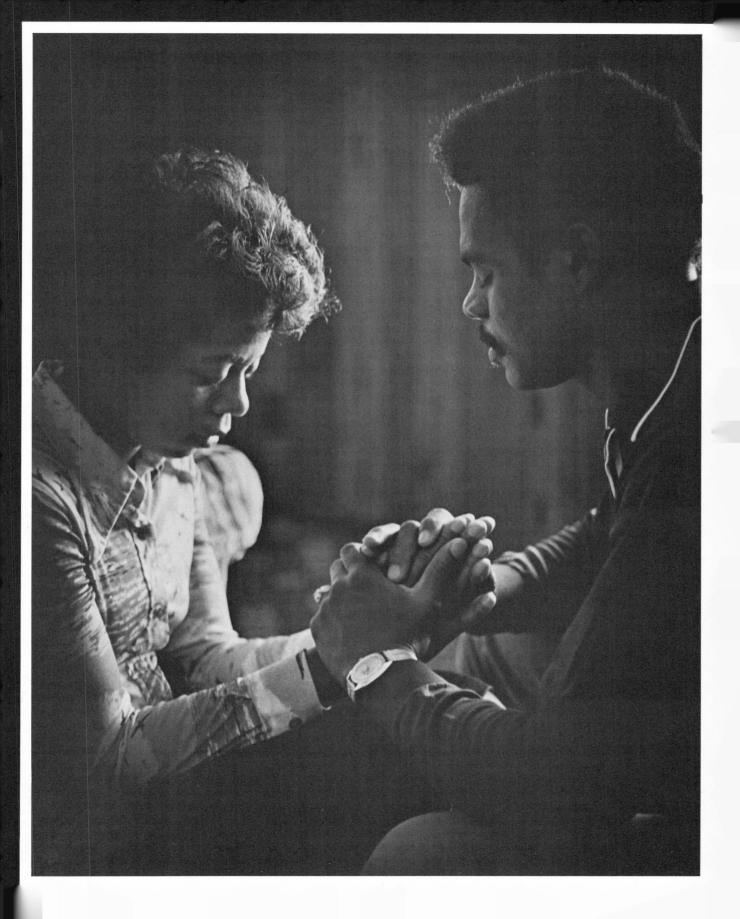

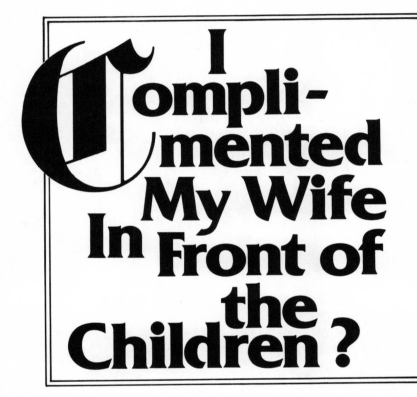

# I Asked My Wife for Her Opinion on a Decision I Had To Make ?

# Passionate Love To My Wife ?

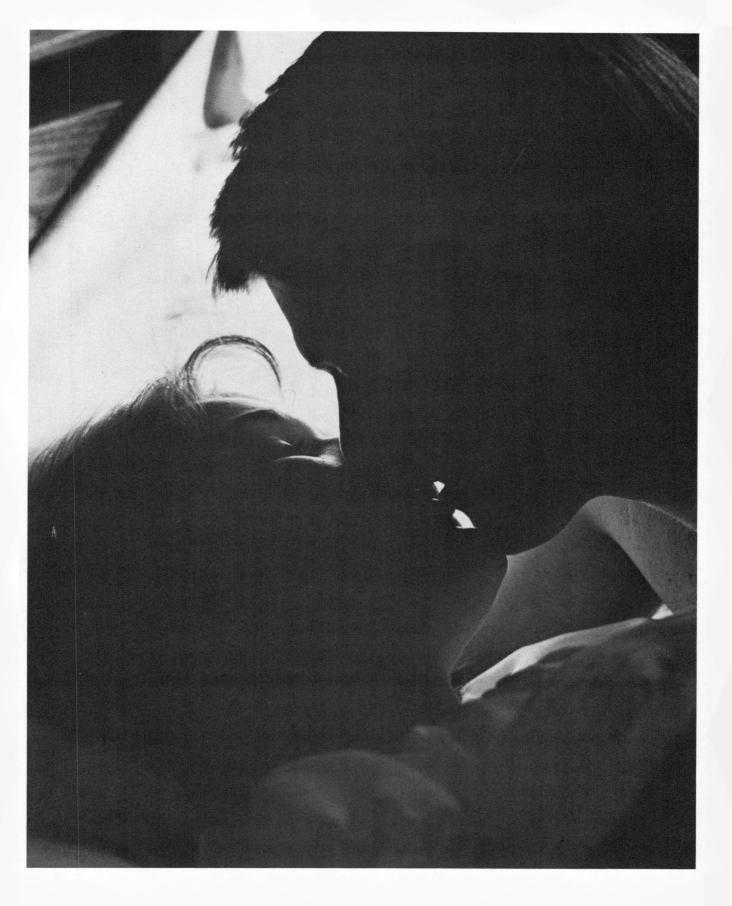

# I Asked One of My Children Out for Coke and Conversation?

# I Fixed a Meal?

# I Balanced the Check-book?

# I Disciplined the Children?

# Dinner with My Family?

# I Asked My Wife What I Could Do To Be a Better Husband?

# I Opened the Door for My Wife?

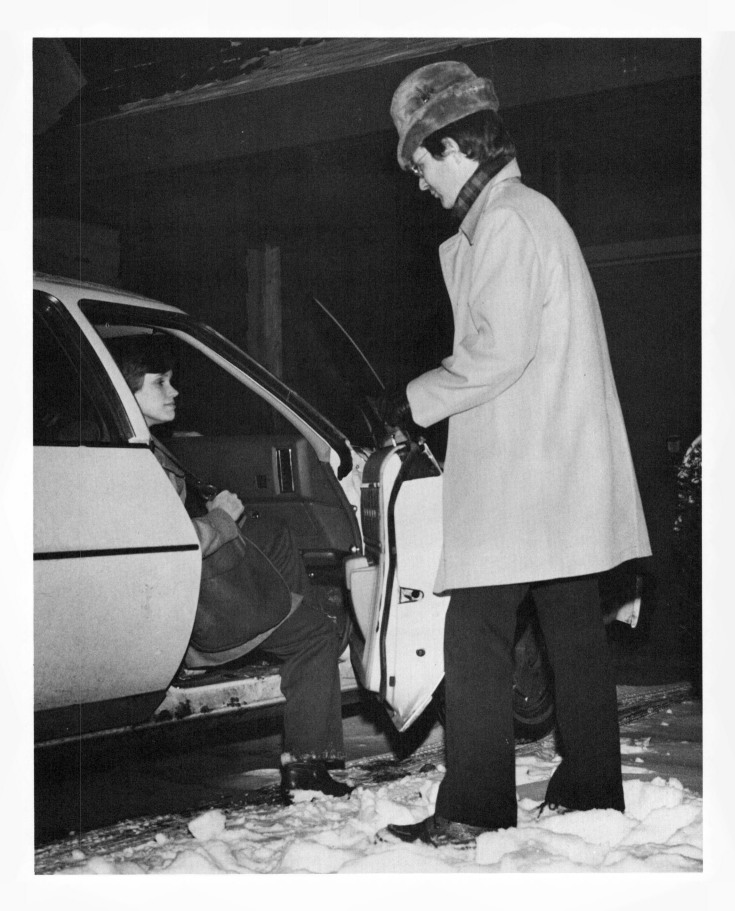

# I Asked My Wife for a Date?

# I Told My Wife I Loved Her More than My Mother ?

# I Gave My Wife $20 and Told Her to Spend It on Herself?

I Did the Chores Around the House Without Being Asked Several Times?

# I Sent My Wife a Flower ?

# I Spent an Evening with My Family with the TV Off?

# I Called My Wife from Work and Told Her She Was Special?

# I Took My Wife On a Week-end Trip Alone ?

# I Prayed with My Children ?

I Held
My Wife
and Told
Her How
Fortunate
I Was To
Have
Married
Her?

**I Asked My Children What Was Happening in Their Lives ?**

**Listened?**

# I Loved and Believed In Myself?

# I Did Not Throw the Past Up To My Wife?

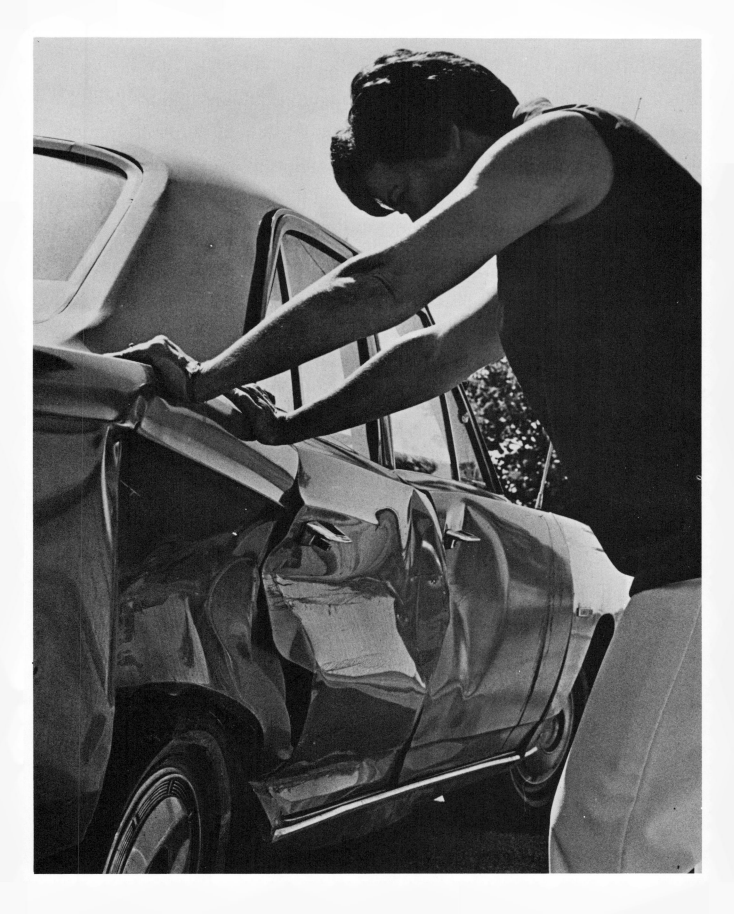

# Read the Bible to the Family with Love and Understanding?

# I Asked God To Guide Me as a Husband and Father ?

I Told
My Wife
I
Loved
Her ?

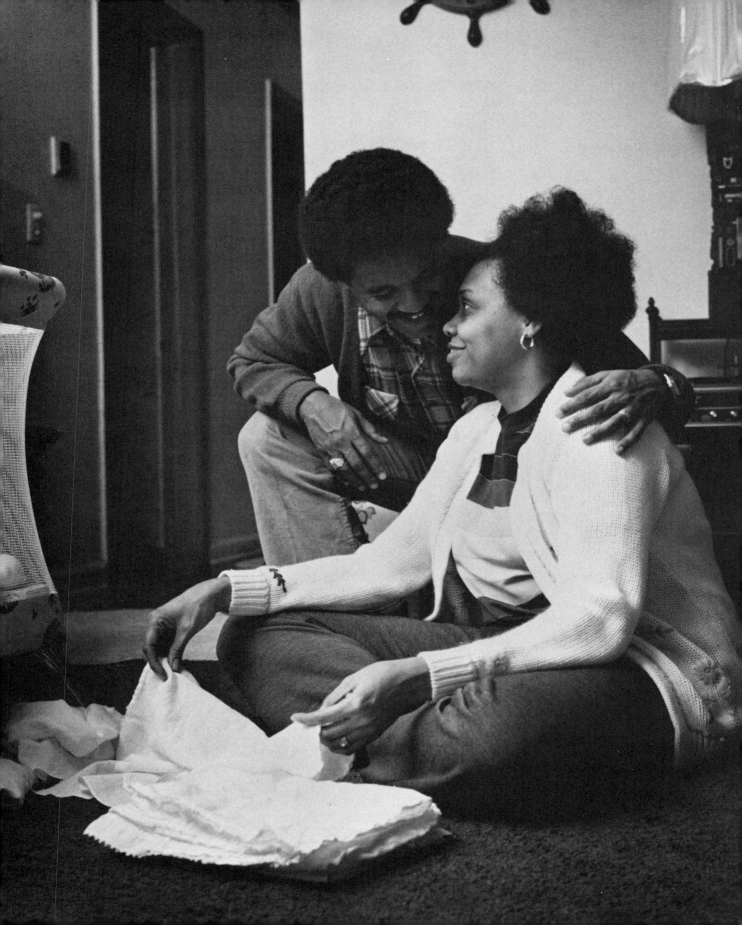

# SELF·EVALUATION

The following inventory is a self-evaluation of your relationship to your wife. Circle the number in front of the statement which best estimates your frequency of doing that particular behavior. For example: 0, 1, 2, 3, 4—I prayed with my wife. If you prayed with your wife one time in the last 12 months circle the 1.

Respond in like manner to all 46 statements and then total your score. Have a friend of yours or several friends take the inventory and compare your results. For your convenience you may wish to record your score below with the date and reexamine yourself yearly or monthly and measure your progress.

Date and result of self-evaluation:

Date _____ Score_____

Date _____ Score_____

Date _____ Score_____

Date _____ Score_____

Date _____ Score_____

# SELF·EVALUATION

| Circle Response: | | | | | |
|---|---|---|---|---|---|
| TIMES LAST 12 MOS. | | | | Or More | Rate yourself and compare your score with a friend's results. |

| | | | | | |
|---|---|---|---|---|---|
| 0 | 1 | 2 | 3 | 4 | I prayed with my wife? |
| 0 | 1 | 2 | 3 | 4 | I complimented my wife in front of the children? |
| 0 | 1 | 2 | 3 | 4 | I cleaned the bathroom? |
| 0 | 1 | 2 | 3 | 4 | I asked my wife for her opinion on a decision I had to make? |
| 0 | 1 | 2 | 3 | 4 | I went to church with my family? |
| 0 | 1 | 2 | 3 | 4 | I kissed my wife without sex as the object? |
| 0 | 1 | 2 | 3 | 4 | I complimented my wife? |
| 0 | 1 | 2 | 3 | 4 | I made passionate love to my wife? |
| 0 | 1 | 2 | 3 | 4 | I asked one of my children out for a coke and conversation? |
| 0 | 1 | 2 | 3 | 4 | I sent my wife a card with a tender thought? |
| 0 | 1 | 2 | 3 | 4 | I babysat so my wife could have a night out? |
| 0 | 1 | 2 | 3 | 4 | I fixed a meal? |
| 0 | 1 | 2 | 3 | 4 | I went on a vacation with my family? |
| 0 | 1 | 2 | 3 | 4 | I balanced the checkbook? |
| 0 | 1 | 2 | 3 | 4 | I disciplined the children? |
| 0 | 1 | 2 | 3 | 4 | I ate dinner with my family? |
| 0 | 1 | 2 | 3 | 4 | I told my children how special they are? |
| 0 | 1 | 2 | 3 | 4 | I had a good open conversation with my wife? |
| 0 | 1 | 2 | 3 | 4 | I played games with my family? |
| 0 | 1 | 2 | 3 | 4 | I did the grocery shopping? |
| 0 | 1 | 2 | 3 | 4 | I asked my wife what I could do to be a better husband? |
| 0 | 1 | 2 | 3 | 4 | I opened the door for my wife? |
| 0 | 1 | 2 | 3 | 4 | I asked my wife for a date? |

0 1 2 3 4    I told my wife I loved her more than my mother?

0 1 2 3 4    I gave my wife $20.00 and told her to spend it on herself?

0 1 2 3 4    I did my chores around the house without being asked several times?

0 1 2 3 4    I sent my wife a flower?

0 1 2 3 4    I told my wife she was beautiful?

0 1 2 3 4    I spent an evening with my family with the TV off?

0 1 2 3 4    I called my wife from work and told her she was special?

0 1 2 3 4    I took my wife on a week-end trip alone?

0 1 2 3 4    I came home from work and gave everyone a hug?

0 1 2 3 4    I prayed with my children?

0 1 2 3 4    I held my wife and told her how fortunate I was to be married to her?

0 1 2 3 4    I asked my children what was happening in their lives?

0 1 2 3 4    I listened?

0 1 2 3 4    I took my wife for a walk?

0 1 2 3 4    I did the dishes or helped my wife do the dishes?

0 1 2 3 4    I remembered my wife's birthday and our anniversary?

0 1 2 3 4    I loved and believed in myself?

0 1 2 3 4    I did not throw the past up to my wife?

0 1 2 3 4    I asked the blessing at the table?

0 1 2 3 4    I accepted my wife for what she is and let her be herself

0 1 2 3 4    I read the Bible to the family with love and understanding?

0 1 2 3 4    I asked God to guide me as a husband and father?

0 1 2 3 4    I told my wife I loved her?

TOTAL